I AM WITH YOU

Fellowship with the Holy Spirit

Leslie Johnson

Paperback ISBN: 978-1-955605-70-0

Cover and Interior Design: B.O.Y. Enterprises, Inc.

Printed in the United States.

DEDICATION

Wow! Holy Spirit always amazes me when I ask Him specific questions. Who should I dedicate this book to, Holy Spirit? The matriarchs of your mom and dad, He says. Holy Spirit told me this when I started my initial dedication, but somehow, I thought I saved the initial dedication, but obviously, I didn't. Annie Dell Haynesworth is my mom's mother and Hannah Weldon is my dad's mother. Holy Spirit continued to say, they were prayer warriors, just as you are. Everyone is not called and chosen to war in prayer as they have during their time here or have you been in this time. What an honor to be chosen as a prayer warrior! Now, what still amazes me is that both of my grandmothers were born in the same month and year (July 1914), four days apart and they passed at the ages of 94 (Grannie Annie Dale) and 98 (Grannie Hannah). Wouldn't it be like God to see this day before this day? Amazing! It is my honor to dedicate this book to a legacy of prayer warriors and to continue to carry the mantle of this gift. In loving memory of you both. The successor of the promise. I love you.

Leslie (Cookie)

Table of Contents

"Behold, I stand at the door [of the church] and continually knock. If anyone hears My voice and opens the door, I will come in and eat with him (restore him), and he with Me." **-Revelations 3:20 (AMP)**

INTRODUCTION

Some address God as "God", yet some as "Holy Spirit". Well, I have learned that He is both, but the roles can be different for every believer of Jesus Christ. You know, Jesus Christ, the Son of God. Jesus Christ, the Savior of the world who came in the likeness of God Himself on the earth to be an example or representative of His Father in Heaven. As Jesus Christ was on earth, He experienced what we experience and pleased His Father in Heaven. In doing as His Father said in obedience to the will of His Father (God), He was crucified on the cross for the sake of our lives so that we can live again from the penalty of sin that was designed for us through Adam. Because of this intervention, the Holy Spirit was given to and for us as a Helper in all matters in our lives.

My relationship with Holy Spirit has been a journey of learning who God is and who I am in Him. By the leading of the Holy Spirit and my obedience to Him, the word apathy (a form of depression) was given to me when I did not know what was happening to me. I was not aware of what the word meant until Holy Spirit spoke to me about it. He told me what to do for my deliverance and then He would tell me when it was trying to return but gave another word for it – lethargy. These words are not for everyday use, so I knew it was His voice speaking to me. He (Holy Spirit) also told me where it came from. He is the Spirit of Truth and knows ALL things. He also allowed me to share it with someone else because they too were experiencing the same. Through the leading of the Holy Spirit, we must always share with others that they too can ask the Holy Spirit for specifics for their lives.

I desire that everyone who reads this book of devotion would encounter and experience the Holy Spirit in such a way that they themselves are walking with Jesus Christ, just as the disciples did. We too, are His disciples. As you read of my encounters with the Holy Spirit, I pray you also have your own personal encounters that will release the specifics you need for your life. Happy reading and growing!

PART 1

LAYING A FOUNDATION FOR RELATIONSHIP WITH THE HOLY SPIRIT

A Firm Foundation

A few years ago, the ministry that my husband and I attended split or shut down. What I experienced was of course not what others did. My question was, did anyone or was anyone really surprised? I have always believed that God/Holy Spirit always reveals signs or has spoken directly to someone because He is the Spirit of truth and there is nothing hidden that He will not make known (Mark 4:22, Luke 8:17). It is said that everyone welcomes or accepts the truth, but that is not true.

Now, my husband had already left the ministry before the church meeting took place that exposed the truth. It was presented prior to this to leadership, that if anyone was doing ministry for the sake of the pastor and not for God, then to give up any keys and/or come talk with the pastor. This was a "way of escape" for my husband, and he took it. He had been tired for a long time with the responsibilities he had. My only regret was not leaving before it all happened.

Even though it was a foundation that was in my life, it was also a foundation that was not there anymore. This is also evidence that you should have your true foundation in God. Foundations are the core of things we build upon and when it is not there, everything that you built on it is gone....part of your finances, part of your time (or a lot of time), part of your children's lives, and half of your life it seems. We do make ministry the center of our lives because this is where we BEGAN A CHANGE in our lives to live for Christ. But make no mistake, as we grow in Christ, He becomes our firm foundation. When everything around you fails, Christ will be the solid rock on which you stand.

Reflection

Can you recall a time when it seems as though your foundation crumbled? How did you handle it? How is the Holy Spirit guiding you to your firm foundation?

_____

_____

_____

_____

_____

_____

_____

_____

_____

_____

_____

_____

_____

_____

_____

SUPPORT

Now, before the shutdown of the ministry, I was already dealing with identity issues. I cannot say when it began but always believed that I needed to find out but just could not pinpoint it. I would ask the Holy Spirit and share it with others, but nothing would come to me or through others. Others would give what they thought it was, but it was never a certainty in their words. When I finally received an answer from the Holy Spirit, he said that it began when my husband did not support me when I ventured to be a travel agent. The key word was "Support".

He had always supported me in whatever I did and encouraged me as well prior to this. He had considered joining me in this venture, but he needed proof or testimonies that money can be earned in traveling. So, he attended an event to hear for himself from others that prospered or were successful. He agreed to partner with me, and it was set up by my leaders at the event, but he changed his mind. I didn't think or feel anything at the time. I continued with the travel agent venture. There was also an annual convention that I attended, and it was an amazing experience.

I think I may have stayed in it for a year or less (not sure), but never-the-less, it did not last long. It was something I stepped out on just in case it was what the Lord was leading me to do.

Let's talk about "Support". I knew and know that support is important because this is how God created us to be. To help, encourage and be there for each other. With that being said, I learned that when that "support" is not there, it's as the scripture says, "There are many members, but one body. And the eye cannot say to the hand I have no need of you, nor the head to feet, I have no need of you. All parts are necessary (1 Corinthians 12:20-22 NKJV). And Ephesians 4:16 says that the whole body is joined together and held together as each does its supporting part that it grows and builds itself in love.

Reflection

How important is support to you in your relationships?

_____

_____

_____

_____

Are you able to remain in relationships with people who do not support your dreams and goals?

_____

_____

_____

_____

What role does support play in the function of the local church?

_____

_____

_____

_____

FOUNDATION AND SUPPORT

S upport is a foundation that gives what is needed in whatever aspect to build. Good intentional support will be there during the duration that it is needed or willed even if it is only for a shorter period of time. However, if needed or willed again, it will return without delay or hesitation.

Sometimes, when we set our intentions to support others, we can stay beyond the prescribed period of time God has set for us. When this happens, we begin to see the crumbling of foundations I mentioned in a previous entry. Supporting beyond what God intends can lead to missed opportunities for growth and advancement and lead to stagnation. Stagnation leads to poverty IN THE MIND. Your will be done is what we need to say sometimes and allow the Holy Spirit to lead and strengthen you to do what is being asked. Ephesians 2:13 says for it is God who works in you **both to will and to do** for *His* good pleasure.

You supporting the person or ministry you have been assigned to is for God's good pleasure. You staying beyond the time God has assigned is no longer support, it is remaining stagnant in a crumbling foundation.

Reflection

Have you ever stayed in a place longer than God graced you to remain? What were the consequences? How did you realign with God's plan for your life?

_____

_____

_____

_____

_____

_____

_____

_____

_____

_____

_____

_____

_____

_____

_____

ONENESS

Fellowship is oneness with another. This is the definition of fellowship, or rather part of, as the Holy Spirit gave to me. Oneness is also what the Holy Spirit **wants** with us. He wants and desires this with us. Just as Jesus was one with the Father, He desires oneness with us through Jesus Christ. Oneness, together, in agreement. Things are so much better this way. Intimacy is what God desires. He knows us, but do we know Him? To love Him is to know Him. He loves us. He loves me. I have heard this from a dear sister in Christ on two occasions unexpectedly or unaware after talking with her. I needed to hear these words during those occasions.

This is how the Holy Spirit moves through those who are obedient to his voice, which is also is an example of oneness with His Spirit. John 3:8 says, "The **wind** blows where it wishes, and you hear the sound of it, but cannot tell where it comes from and where it goes. So is everyone who is born of the **Spirit**." When my dear sister in Christ was reminding me that The Father loves me, she was operating in obedience to His word and displaying her Oneness with the Holy Spirit by following His prompting.

Reflection

What does Oneness with the Holy Spirit mean to you?

_____

_____

_____

_____

_____

_____

_____

_____

_____

_____

_____

_____

_____

_____

_____

LOVE

1 John 5:3 says, *"For this is the love of God, that we keep His commandments. And His commandments are not **burdensome**."* This means obedience to His word is not hard. I remember asking my husband to live with me with understanding (1 Peter 3:7) while I gather the fragments of my life. This is during the time that I was struggling with my identity in Christ. He didn't understand. How could he when he too was broken? This is why it is vital to have consistent intimacy with the Holy Spirit and know His love for you. It was love that died for me. Who would not love someone who gave His life for them? Some find it difficult. I needed to find that love again.

Without love, we are lost and feel alone even when we are around others. It's amazing even to think that someone loves you. It's that missing part in your life that only LOVE can fill. Let's consider the life of Nicodemus who went to Jesus by night and acknowledged who Jesus was, but he did not know that Jesus was the very essence of love. Nicodemus knew the Law but did not know love. He was missing love. I will not be a scribe of God's word and not know God's love! My life is at stake, and it should be because ALL was placed on the stake of the Cross for me and for you. The cost of the love of God cannot be measured with anything in the entire world, no matter how much it cost. I don't want to be or feel lonely again because saying I'm lonely is the same thing as saying I am without Jesus Christ.

To be lonely is to be without Jesus Christ.

"I am with you," says the Holy Spirit. "Come, get to know me in a deeper way. I will fill every void in your life. There is no fear in my love. I will remove all fear and fill you with my love. Come, learn of me. I love you. You don't have to wait to see if I am available. I am ALWAYS available. When you find me, you find you. You are the apple of my eye. I have no jealousy. I do not compete. As a matter of fact, I made you to love and to love others."

Reflection

What comes to your mind when you hear the word "Love"?

_____

_____

_____

_____

_____

_____

Re-read the Holy Spirit's message to you on the previous page and write your response below.

_____

_____

_____

_____

_____

_____

_____

SUBMISSION

I heard the Lord say to me, "Now is the time for you to do my will in full submission." That sounded great, but I immediately questioned whether or not I really know what full submission is? We hear to give ALL to God, but HOW do we get to the full submission? Have I ever heard really good teaching on the full submission? "Seek and you shall find, says that Holy Spirit. What you seek or look for will be drawn to you."

Before we dig deeper into submission, I will say this. Don't ever lose your hunger for God. Do what is necessary or required to stay consistent and submitted. After you have tasted and seen that the Lord is good and then lose that taste (zeal, hunger), it's a challenge to get back. Some have said that all you have to do is this and that. It's not a simple "all you have to do". People don't want to be honest because of shame or maybe even entitlement. I don't know but it is a challenge. This is whether you fell and submitted yourself back to your former life or you haven't made time to pray or be consistent in prayer, read the word of God, or fellowship with other believers. A fall is a fall.

Some falls are more damaging than others, just as in the physical nature. All falls experience some sort of trauma. Trauma is an emotional response to a distressing event or experience. Shock and denial are typical. These emotions can affect relationships as well. Emotions can be unpredictable and there are flashbacks of the experience. It can also shatter your sense of security (no longer confident, feeling helpless). A common saying during these "emotional seasons" is I am okay, but you are not. Falls can lead to injuries that, if not properly treated, can interfere with your submission to God and His word. This is why is so important to have a relationship with God and if needed an accountability partner that you can trust fully.

With your relationship with God (the Holy Spirit), He knows you better than anyone else. Even your mother. Yes, the one that bore you. God is your Creator. He knew you would experience what you did and guess what? He has all the answers. God loves you so much that He gave His only Son, Jesus Christ that the world is saved through Him. To know this is amazing, but sometimes during your trauma season, you can't seem to bring yourself to believe it. Relationship/intimacy is what God desires from His creation. Intimacy with God requires your full submission to Him. Once intimacy begins, we then find out who we are and what we are able to do for Him and others. Your submission to God is the starting point for His destiny to be revealed in your life.

Reflection

What does submission to God look like in your life?

_____

_____

_____

_____

_____

_____

_____

_____

How has submission to God changed your life and your relationships with others?

_____

_____

_____

_____

_____

PART 2

A DEEPER RELATIONSHIP

RELATIONSHIP

What is a relationship? It's a commitment between two people who decided to be loyal to one another. That's a basic textbook definition, but do we truly know what a relationship is? A relationship does involve a connection of two, whether it be people, concepts, or objects. With this being said, a connection is for purpose, but if one person, concept, or object does not do their part, then purpose does not happen. All can be present, but nothing happens. The same is true in our relationship with Holy Spirit. The principle of fellowship is "oneness" with another ACTIVELY, meaning both parties must actively engage in order for the relationship to be fruitful. So why doesn't everyone want to have a relationship with the Holy Spirit, the very essence of God, our Creator?

Sometimes we can get so caught up in the mechanics of relationship like asking God a question and expecting an immediate answer, that we box ourselves into a pattern of stagnation. Even while writing this book, there were moments when I asked God what to write and did not initially hear a response. I wanted to be led a particular way, but when I put my pretense to the side and decided to just "BE" in the presence of God, the answers began to flow through my fingers and onto the pages.

That's what you need to do," Just Be" and do what is needed to connect with God. Will you just sit and do nothing, or will you ACTIVELY try to connect with God when you do not hear Him? In those moments during my writing process, Holy Spirit said to me, "Everything you need is in you, in spite of your outside relationships that did not go well. I Am with you. Remember, I stand at the door and knock to come in (Revelation 3:20). I want and desire to come into what I created for my purpose and for yours. There is so much I want to show and do through you. Eye has not seen, nor ear has not heard nor **has** entered into the heart of man the things which God has prepared for those who love Him." (1 Corinthians 2:9). Oh my beloved, great and mighty things I can show you that you do not know (Jeremiah 33:3). Come closer to me and I will show you more."

Reflection

In the previous devotional entry, I shared with you how my relationship with the Holy Spirit flows when I learn to "just be" in His presence. Take a few moments to sit in His presence, then use the space below to write what you sense, see, and feel in your spirit.

_____

_____

_____

_____

_____

_____

_____

_____

_____

_____

_____

_____

_____

_____

_____

A Prayer of Thanks and Surrender

Thank you for loving me! Thank you for choosing me! Thank you for delivering me! Thank you for saving me, even now! Thank you for protecting me! Thank you for restoring me! Thank you for healing me! Thank you, thank you, thank you, Lord! Thank you for being my Savior, Lover, Counselor, and Sustainer! There is no one like you Lord! You are my Redeemer! I love you!

Thank you for anointing me for Your purpose! Help me to please you in all things. I can't do it on my own. I belong to you, so I need you to help me. Help me to trust you. Teach me how to love me. Create in me a clean heart and renew a right spirit within me (Psalms 51:10). No more residue that would contaminate me from moving forward in you. Give me wisdom for what you want me to do for you. I want to do it with your love. Your will be done in me. You are my shepherd. I lack nothing. You have given me everything I need. Now, teach me how to access it fully, with confidence, boldness, authority, power with joy. You are my strength, peace, joy, love, hope, and security. All things were made by you and for you. I surrender to your will for my life, in Jesus' name, amen.

Reflection

Use the space below to write your own prayer of thanks to God.

_____

_____

_____

_____

_____

_____

_____

_____

_____

_____

_____

_____

_____

_____

_____

_____

_____

_____

_____

_____

_____

SPIRIT AND TRUTH

As I sat down to write this devotional, the Holy Spirit said to me, "All things are composed in my Spirit and in my Truth. It's a place of liberty and freedom. To know me in Spirit, you know me by my truth, because my spirit directs into all truth. ALL. That means in ALL of your life, every area, every relationship. By me everything was made; visible and invisible. I know ALL. No one can hide. Draw/come closer to me. I will teach you, tell you, and guide you in who I am and who you are. I will tell you what you were created for in this life. Let me show you. I love you. There is no other love as my love. In my love is peace. In my love is joy. In my love is strength. In my love, you can rest and know that I AM always with you. I will tell you things you do not know. By the way, in my love is protection. COME. Walk with me. I am here for you. I LOVE YOU. I will perfect those things that concern you. Learn of me and I will give you rest, my beloved."

Reflection

In the devotional you just read, the Holy Spirit encouraged you to draw closer to Him. Write your response to Him below.

_____

_____

_____

_____

_____

_____

_____

_____

_____

_____

_____

_____

_____

_____

_____

_____

_____

_____

_____

A CONVERSATION WITH THE HOLY SPIRIT

The entry you are about to read is a conversation between the Holy Spirit and me. It is a deeply intimate display of the care and concern He has for all of us. I pray you are encouraged to go deeper in conversation with Him in your daily life as you read what transpired between the two of us.

"I love you, my beloved. Know that you are on my mind and in my heart always. I so care for you to help you and keep you in the way of righteousness. What joy that was set before me to give my life for you. There was no shame. Let me truly be the author and finisher of your faith daily. I know your ending before your beginning. I was in the beginning and will be the ending of all things upon the earth. Let me help you in all matters. Tell me what you desire. Walk with me more. Listen for my directions. My paths are of peace and purpose. Fearfully and wonderfully, I have made you. My prized creation I have made you to be; to be like me. You have done well with stepping out again. Know that I am still with you, even when you are not sure. I know you long to hear me more. Step, step, step, move, move, move. I will not let you stumble or fall. I hear your heart's desires when you do not speak. Your firsts in this session will end in greatness. Remember, I know the ending before the beginning. **Breathe, step, move**. Trust what's in you."

"How do I do that, Lord? I hear that from others when there is uncertainty, but at the same time, I want to be sure it's what's supposed to be done. To be sure is knowing it's the right decision without it being a wasteful or incorrect decision."

"How will you learn," says the Holy Spirit?

31

"You said to take your yoke upon me and learn of you (Matthew 11:29)."

"Yes, that is true but how will you learn? Remember breathe, step, and move. What if that next move would open a portal that breaks every cycle that tries to keep recurring? Did you see the word I used at the end of the breathe, step, and **move**? I know the ending before the beginning. Do not focus on the beginning. The end (the move) will end cycles, the end will bring peace, and continuous joy (that's the unspeakable joy, too), it will plummet you into what's always been in you. The very desires you have not found yet, but the yearning is there. **Breathe, step, move.** You are my workmanship (Ephesians 2:10). I am the Potter you are the clay. I am making another (a new) vessel (Jeremiah 18:1-4). Your pinnacles will be of rubies (Isaiah 54:12)."

Reflection

God is always looking for opportunities to fellowship with you. Create an atmosphere of worship in your home, then use the space below to record your conversation with the Holy Spirit.

_____

_____

_____

_____

_____

_____

_____

_____

_____

_____

_____

_____

_____

_____

_____

_____

_____

_____

_____

_____

VENTURING INTO THE UNCHARTED

The Holy Spirit says, "Trusting me is essential to where I am taking you. Uncharted places and people. Hear my voice and take heed (give attention to). I will give the way to walk in when you turn to the right hand or to the left (Isaiah 30:21). Venture. Uncharted ventures are not traveled, unfamiliar or unknown places. Deep calls unto deep. No more shallow waters. Move from the shores of complacency/common knowings. Obey. I am with you. I am and will set the right people in place. I will prepare the way. Remember, I am the truth, the way, and the life (John 14:6). Peace, I give you (John 14:27). The journey. Seek me more. You will need it for the journey. Travail. Certain pursuits are not necessary. They are not meaningful or purposeful. [Restoration is coming and has already begun. I will do with you as I did with Elijah. I will make provision for the journey in the uncharted places. (1 King 17)

You are mine. I will make a way in the wilderness (Isaiah 43:19). Trust me. Know me more. I will put words in your mouth. Know that I am God. You are my conduit in the earth."

Reflection

The Holy Spirit just ministered to you regarding the "Uncharted". What does that word mean to you and what is He saying to you specifically about venturing into the uncharted?

_____

_____

_____

_____

_____

_____

_____

_____

_____

_____

_____

_____

_____

_____

_____

_____

_____

_____

_____

PREREQUISITE

Prerequisite- that which is required before anything else can happen. Sometimes we just need to just DO what is needed or even expected. Having expectation is good, but with that, the work needs to be done. Faith without works is dead, just as the body without the Spirit of God is dead (James 2:20, 26). Spiritual death is a life without God, but what is more important, is a relationship with God through the Holy Spirit. Not just a shallow relationship, meaning having the knowledge of, but not the intimacy of (oneness with the person of the Holy Spirit). Letting Him teach you, guide you, comfort you, protect you, heal you, tell you who He is and who you truly are. This is a lifetime relationship that is prerequisite for a purposeful life that you were created for. Old ways and old habits of doing things are changed as you draw near to God and learn of Him and learn of you. Your mind is renewed. And as your mind is renewed, your behavior changes for that which is good through the righteousness of God.

A lifetime relationship with the Holy Spirit

The Holy Spirit is the Spirit of God. It's the Spirit of truth in all matters of life. Wouldn't you want to know the matters of your life and the answers of why things happen or even not happen? This lifetime relationship is available to all without partiality. Come to me all that are weary and heavy laden, and I will give you rest (Matthew 11:28).

Everything you are believing God for, will happen once you fulfill the prerequisite of a lifetime relationship with Him.

Reflection

Have you committed to a lifetime relationship with the Holy Spirit? What evidence of this commitment is seen in your daily life?

_____

_____

_____

_____

_____

_____

_____

_____

_____

_____

_____

_____

_____

_____

_____

_____

_____

_____

YOU ARE A UNIQUE CREATION

(God's message to His creation)

I will show you the way. The way is my will, thoughts, plan, guidance, voice, peace, joy; no one else but who I created you to be. I do not make or create clones. No one person is like another. Your making is unique. Carbon copies are not my specialty. You are special, peculiar, a royal priesthood, but not like another (1 Peter 2:9); a chosen vessel for honor for the master's use (2 Timothy 2:21).

I take pleasure in my creation. I desire for them to please me. I actually created you to please me. You are able to do all that I have created you to do. It's within you. You are never lost of who you are. Some feel lost because they have taken on someone else's making, so I have to get them back on the potter's wheel to make another vessel (Jeremiah 18:4); the one I created in the beginning. I placed eternity in man, so they will know that they have a Creator not made by man's hand or even man's ideas/thoughts (Ecclesiastes 3:11; 2 Corinthians 5:1). I am always drawing my creation back to me. They just do not draw closer to me when I draw them. I love my creation. My love is so unconditional that it cannot be denied, but it is in the perception of man. I always have your best interest at heart because you have been created in my image and likeness. This is why man cannot deny their true Creator. They can try but within, they know.

Reflection

God created you as a unique expression of Himself. Use the space below to write your thoughts about your uniqueness and the intentionality of God as He created you.

_____

_____

_____

_____

_____

_____

_____

_____

_____

_____

_____

_____

_____

_____

_____

_____

_____

_____

_____

_____

AN ENCOUNTER WITH LOVE

We need an encounter of your love. (This was a verse of the song I was listening to as I wrote this). Lord, Your love is unexplainable, unshakable and irresistible. We can know this, but to be intimate with your love is a different experience. To love you is to obey you. That's what you say in your word. You said if I (we) love you, keep your commandments (John 14:15). Commandments are instructions from your word by principle, knowledge or by your spirit. Now, the leading of your Holy Spirit is personal and may not be scriptural. It's obeying what you speak to us (this is still a commandment to do).

I read Revelations 3 and heard the Holy Spirit say, Repent and turn from your ways and your thoughts. I stand at the door and knock. Open that I may come in to dine with you; talk with you. I am here; take heed to what I want to tell you. Know me, not just "of" me. I am your life. I know what is best for you. Turn, turn, turn, now. Beloved, turn, hear and do what I command. My lovingkindness is better than life. I know the thoughts that I think toward you, says the Lord, thoughts of peace and not of evil, to give you a future and a hope (Jeremiah 29:11). Hope that does not disappoint as man does. A future abundantly on this earth and eternal when you leave this earth. Come.

Reflection

What does an encounter with the Love of God look like to you?

_____

_____

_____

_____

_____

_____

_____

_____

How can you create time and opportunity to encounter the Love of God in your everyday life?

_____

_____

_____

_____

_____

_____

_____

OBEDIENCE IS LOVE

Obedience is the act of doing what is spoken; a willingness of doing what is said. This is the requirement to show me that you love me, as my word says, if you love me, do as I command. Love and obedience work together to demonstrate that you are my disciple, a follower and a doer of my word. My word is not burdensome, but the way of a transgressor is hard (difficult). A transgressor is someone who is not willing to obey in the way of my word. There are so many blessings, benefits and rewards with obeying my word. My word demonstrates my love to you by protecting you, saving you, healing you, delivering you, giving you joy, peace, assurance, and strength.

You are my most prized possession that I created. I love you with an everlasting love. No one can love you as I love you. You can search everywhere, and you will not find a love like mine. I gave my life because of my love for you. I then walked the earth to show who I was and who I am. I walked the earth to show my compassion, power, authority, provision and protection. I walked the earth to show that you too can do as I did, but greater. I chose you to be an example of my love and work. I am not like man. I change not. I am true to my word because I am the word. Nothing can compare to the many facets of my word. I have called you to liberty and freedom. I called you by name. I knew you before you were born. My thoughts for you were already planned. I used man to bring you forth. It was their purpose to bring you into this world. Their purposes are not the same as yours. Some aspects may seem the same, but it's not. To know me is to love me. Come closer to me and I will come closer to you. There is no fear in me. I am gentle in heart, and I am able to carry any burdens you have.

Reflection

The Word of God tells us to love Him is to obey Him. What, if anything, do you need to adjust to strengthen your walk of obedience?

_____

_____

_____

_____

_____

_____

_____

_____

Have you considered what it means to be God's most prized creation? Ponder on that thought for a moment and write what you sense, feel, and hear below.

_____

_____

_____

_____

_____

GOD'S MESSAGE OF BREAKTHROUGH

This is your season for breakthrough. Believe and trust me totally. I know it's been a challenge, but I am still with you. Not just the passive "I am with", this is the intimate "I am with you". I know it may not feel like it, but it is intimate. You are experiencing the pureness of it that you have not before. This is why it seems as though I am not with you.

This part of your journey will break every stronghold in your life and life of your family. The battle is not all yours. Let me fight it. You were just told that the battle was not yours. Hear what my Spirit is saying to you. I will teach you how to war when it's time. But not now. I will give you instructions. Only a few will have access to you. I will sharpen your ears to hear me with clarity. The key is to rest in me and know that I am with you. I love you so much.

I am loosing you as you walk with me. I will tell you when to walk away, when to speak, and when not to speak. No more clamor (a loud and confusing noise). I am silencing every clamor. In my presence is fullness of joy. You will have the fullness of my joy, greater than before! All will see. The heaviness comes to stifle the joy that IS to come. Stifle means to interrupt or cut off; to repress; keep in or hold back; to smother or suffocate; to die of suffocation. As I told Peter, Satan has asked for you and desires to sift you as wheat, but I have prayed for you, that your faith shall not fail; and when you return to me, strengthen your brethren (Luke 22:31-32). Your story/journey is not exactly as Peter's. You are in the process of being strengthened. Beware of the distractions. They are in forms of stifling disguised. Peter denied me through others, but I need you to deny people's access to you during this time as I strengthen you. I will provide what you need for the journey. Have I not already? You have and will have enough (Luke 22:38). A refreshing. I have come to invade the power of darkness, every principality, power, and wickedness in high places. Gird up your loins with my word and follow my instructions.

Reflection

This is your season for breakthrough. Make a list of the areas of your life you are believing for breakthrough.

_____

_____

_____

_____

_____

_____

_____

_____

_____

_____

_____

_____

_____

_____

TRUST

Trust said the Holy Spirit. It will always be Trust throughout your journey. Trust involves stepping into that which is unfamiliar to you as I lead you; that which is not common to you. It is stepping and walking into who you are if you allow it. There is a fullness and wholeness you will experience. It's a stretching from old to new. Behaviors and thinking are new that may seem uncomfortable but it's actually comfortable in a sense of the true you. There's a settling, a rest in my Spirit.

Reflection

What comes to mind when you think of the word trust? Can you honestly say you trust God fully, with all of you? Ponder these questions and write your responses below.

_____

_____

_____

_____

_____

_____

_____

_____

_____

_____

_____

_____

_____

_____

_____

_____

_____

A Prayer of Adoration and Thanksgiving

There is none like you Lord. Thank you for loving us. Thank you for caring for us. Thank you for protecting us. Thank you for the angels that fulfill their assignments for us. Thank you for all things good and not-so-good. Thank you for your strength. Thank you for your peace. Thank you for your joy. Thank you for the thoughts (plans) you have for us. Thoughts (plans) of good and not evil, that of a future and a hope. Hope in Jesus Christ, our Lord, and Savior. He is the only true Savior of the world. The only true and living God, in Jesus' name, amen.

Reflection

Use the space below to write your own targeted prayer of adoration and thanksgiving.

_____

_____

_____

_____

_____

_____

_____

_____

_____

_____

_____

_____

_____

_____

_____

_____

A HEART'S CRY

Lay aside every weight and sin that so easily ensnares you (Hebrews 12:1). A fresh fire. I need and want to be consumed. No more of me, Lord. Help me to move me out of the way. What are the weights that I have not laid aside? What are my distractions besides myself? I want to please You in every way. No more going through the motions.

I have been placed among various great women on this journey and I am thankful for each one and their part of the assignment. But now, Lord, I really am wanting to be purposeful again. Fulfilled again. Whole again. Where do I begin again? A new thing you said you would do. Then you asked, will you (I) not know it? I have heard you say to me "Now is the time" on a few occasions and then recently. "Arise," you say, for my light has come (Isaiah 60).

Isaiah 54 speaks to me about "crying out" because of bareness. It speaks to me about stretching and letting down my cords. What are the specifics of these scriptures? What do you want me to do? As Paul asked on the road of Damascus, "Lord, what do you want me to do?" (Acts 9:6). I am your servant. I do not want to second guess what you called me to do. I want to be real and honest with others, but still minister your word of truth in an effective way to bring healing and deliverance, to bring hope as you gave me and so many others.

Where do I go from here? I do not want to be stagnant. I do not want to do anything "at random" or anything You do not want me to do. It's time for a hard reset. Not just a "hard reset" for this masterpiece you have orchestrated, but a "heart reset" for me and my life as a servant, a disciple, a mother, a sister in Christ, a believer; an example (the light on the hill, the salt of the earth); the epistle of your word! It's almost as if I need to say, "What must I do to be saved?" An example of the very epitome of Your Love! A living sacrifice as you were. Change me, oh God! You have truly been my present help when I needed even when I was not aware of what you were doing within me.

Reflection

What is your heart's cry? Write it below.

_____

_____

_____

_____

_____

_____

_____

_____

_____

_____

_____

_____

_____

_____

HOW DOES THAT LOOK?

Holy Spirit says, "I need total dependence, my beloved Leslie."

"How does that look Lord?" I asked.

"Lay all at my feet."

"How does that look Lord? My trying to be a perfectionist or trying to do all things right hinders me. It is said we are not perfect. We have that connotation, but I have read in your word that there were some that walked blameless before you and were devout men. There is nothing that says that they made mistakes and had to learn, but if they did it was even before they received the Holy Spirit, we are more able and capable of walking blameless with the Holy Spirit. What am I missing or not doing? Am I doing things/tasks that I am not to do" Now, those can be stumbling blocks that you did not place on me, but stumbles created because of various idols (people, places things) I placed before You. Forgive me Lord. I will not be disqualified. Your word says I can run the race to obtain a crown but still become disqualified if I am not tempered in all things; running with uncertainty and fighting as one who beats the air and not bring my body into discipline and subjection (preaching, ministering) but yet disqualified. (1 Corinthians 9:24-27). I am not to grow or become weary in well doing (Galatians 6:9). Then, 2 Corinthians 13:5 says to examine myself as to whether I am in the faith (test myself). Do I not know that Christ (the Holy Spirit) lives in me? Unless indeed I am disqualified."

Holy Spirits says, "Now fix your crown and get in the race to win as a good soldier."

Reflection

What stumbling blocks or wrong thought patterns have hindered you from "laying all at the feet of Jesus"? After reading this devotional entry, what adjustments do you need to make to get out of your own way?

_____

_____

_____

_____

_____

_____

_____

_____

_____

_____

_____

_____

_____

_____

_____

_____

THE DRAWING OF THE HOLY SPIRIT

Be free! Be free today! Give all to me today. Release it to me now. Learn of me and I will guide you. I will comfort you. I will heal you totally. I will give you joy. I will love you. My love is like none other because I am love. I will teach you and show you how to love the right way. I am your creator. I will not hurt you. I am the same all the time. I do not change. What I say, I will do.

Come to me. Come back to me. I am waiting and have been waiting for my bride. I am your husbandman. I will show you how to be a wife, a husband, a mother, a father, a sister, a brother, a friend, an ambassador, a leader, a conduit for me, and a force not to be reckoned with for others. You are my glory upon the earth. Now, it's not too late to make an impact to those I have assigned to you. I know the heart of man. I can do what I planned for him. I can turn the heart, soften the heart. Even though the heart is deceitful above all things, I can change the heart.

Come to me with all your heart. Do not try to understand with your mind. I am here and will not leave you. Let me love you. Let me fill every void. Your past is just your history and not your present. Accept my gift now. My gift of life. I am in the shattered and broken. I can handle all that you have and had.

Reflection

The Holy Spirit is calling you to a deeper, more intimate relationship with Him. Take a moment to set an atmosphere of worship, then ask the Lord what His call to deeper intimacy means for your life. Record His response below.

_____

_____

_____

_____

_____

_____

_____

_____

_____

_____

_____

_____

_____

_____

_____

REJECTING REJECTION

Did you know that fear causes you to draw away from the help that God has appointed in your life? You may not be aware that you are doing it, but it comes in subtle ways like, "I'm okay", I don't need anything, "I'm good", "I'm just going to stay in", "never mind". The more you do it, the more you will not recognize who is sent to help, because you have rejected all due to the rejection and abandonment you have felt from others.

What now? Your new beginning is now; accepting now and not rehearsing or thinking on what happened. Your days of rejection are over. Will there be somedays that you think you haven't begun again? Yes, but the Holy Spirit is still there waiting for you to talk to Him. Trust Him. Trust is a must and can be difficult at times but remember that He does not change or leave you abandoned. I am still here. I not in religion. I will teach you and show you what is religion. Take my hand. Let's walk.

Reflection

Have you found yourself rejecting help because you are afraid of being ridiculed or rejected? Use the space below to communicate with the Holy Spirit about this fear and His remedy to help you overcome it.

_____

_____

_____

_____

_____

_____

_____

_____

_____

_____

_____

_____

_____

_____

TRUSTING IN THE HOLY SPIRIT

Holy Spirit said, "I am your help in all things. No matter how big or small. I am your all sufficiency. You have a journey that is marvelous (Psalms 118:23). I am with you. Your steps are ordered by Me regardless of you thinking that you are not on the right path. My thoughts or ways are not like yours. Everything I created is good. You are that good part. Because I know your thoughts before you think them, do not wonder if you are overthinking. I am expanding your thoughts as you walk with me and think on me.

I am your peace when chaos is all around. I am your joy when your heart gets a little heavy. Rejoice always, my beloved. Go forth in faith, trusting Me as you move forward. I will not let you stumble. Speak as I direct you and ask for help as I lead you to that person. If you miss my leading, it is still a walk of learning my Spirit. All that I have comes from the Father in heaven. I do not do anything without Him telling me. Just as you should not do anything unless I tell you. Do not think it unusual of the things I say. I am with you.

Eye has not seen, or ear heard what I have for those who love me. (1 Corinthians 2:9) Let me teach you how to truly love. Trust me. I love you with an everlasting love. (Jeremiah 31:3) That's a long time, right? There is no fear in love. Anything that is of fear is torment and does not know my love (1 John 4:18). My love abounds in and over all things. My love covers a multitude of (many) sins (1 Peter 4:8). My love cast out (removes) fear (1 John 4:8). Love me and I will manifest myself to you (John 14:21). I will show you great and mighty things that you do not know (Jeremiah 33:3). Trusting me pleases me because you are trusting me by faith. As you trust me and obey, I will show you who you really are. I will show you your purpose (reason) for living."

Reflection

Take a moment to meditate on the devotional entry you just read. Use the space below to write your response to the Holy Spirit.

HOLY SPIRIT'S EXHORTATION

Freely give as I have given to you, it's bigger than you can imagine. Live the abundant life that I have called you to. Little is much in my hand. Always show up for the assignment. I am your shepherd, your helper, your guide. I am with you. The journey is prepared. Walk as I lead. Be confident knowing it is me that is directing you in all paths of righteousness. No weapon formed against you will prosper. I am your shield and buckler. I will protect you on all sides. Draw closer to me and I will draw closer to you. Call upon me while I am near. The hour is coming when no man will be able to find me. I am coming soon. Do the work that I have called you to do whole heartedly. Know that many are called, but few have been chosen.

My word is essential in this time. Know my word. Fear not, because fear is not of my Spirit. I have not given you the spirit of fear but of love, power, and a sound mind. Couple these with your faith. Be the epistle before all. Every creed, every nation. There is no religion that is more prevalent than the Gospel. No man knows the day or the hour. Prepare for my coming. No delays or hesitations. No procrastination. No doubt, just trust. Trust me in and for all things. Come, let's go to the other side.

Reflection

How does it feel to be nudged by the Holy Spirit? Write your response to His exhortation below.

_____

_____

_____

_____

_____

_____

_____

_____

_____

_____

_____

_____

_____

_____

_____

_____

_____

DEEPER REVELATION

Discard. That was the word the Lord spoke to me. I immediately asked Him what it meant, and He responded with, "It means to get rid of; not to have any association with anymore."

As you continue to deepen your relationship with the Holy Spirit you will notice there will be times that He only gives you just one word to see if you will ask or seek Him for more. Then, if you ask, He will tell you. Sometimes it's an immediate answer. Sometimes He will see if you will continue to seek Him for the meaning or what it is related to. Sometimes it will be made known through other means, such as people, places, or things, but you will need to be sensitive to His spirit to recognize it, that's if you have not forgotten the word that was given. Because He is trying to get you to come closer to Him to seek Him and have a desire for a relationship with Him, He will draw you to that very "attention-getter".

He always wants to bring you into truth, so that you are made free from an area that you may not be aware of due to accepting it as normal, but it's an area of confinement. It can be something as simple as a certain belief that you have always known and accepted as truth, but it's not truth. It's a belief passed on for a long time.

Attachments that do not produce fruitfulness need to be discarded. Ask the Holy Spirit to show you the hidden attachments you have been holding onto. He is the Spirit of truth that knows all things. He can be trusted. Lean not on your own understanding, but in all your ways acknowledge me, says the Holy Spirit. (Proverbs 3:5) I will direct your every path in every area of your life, even NOW. No matter what happened on any day before now. No matter what, no matter who, and no matter how. I will and have the power to forgive you of all. This moment counts NOW.

Now faith (now trust) is the substance [what you are believing me for] of things hoped for [expecting] the evidence [what will be seen as you trust] of things not seen yet (Hebrews 11:1). Trust and obey my promptings, impressions, leading, or directions. There is life from the past that will not help you to a future that will fulfill you. I know it can be a challenge to trust someone you do not physically see, but I am more present than those who you do see. I stand at the door knocking, waiting for you to let me in (Revelation 3:20). I know your ending before the beginning. Who [with reason] despises the day of small things (beginnings)? (Zechariah 4:10).

Reflection

God desires to continue this journey of intimate fellowship with you. As mentioned in the previous entry, the more time you spend in His presence, the deeper your revelation and understanding of His word will be. Use the space below to start a new conversation with the Holy Spirit to help deepen your intimacy with Him.

_____

_____

_____

_____

_____

_____

_____

_____

_____

_____

_____